# Usborne Art Ideas
# Drawing
# Cartoons

INTERNET-LINKED

## Anna Milbourne

Designed by Jan McCafferty and Catherine-Anne MacKinnon

Illustrated by Jan McCafferty, Gary Dunn, Christyan Fox, John Richardson, Paddy Mounter, Catherine-Anne MacKinnon, Sarah McIntyre, Uwe Mayer, Neil Scott, Andy Hammond, David Pattison, Adam Stower, Antonia Miller and Ian McNee

Additional illustrations by Alex de Wolf, Anna Milbourne, Kevin Faerber,
Geo Parker, Stephen Cartwright, Vici Leyhane and Ainsley Knox
Additional design by Andrea Slane, Antonia Miller and Vici Leyhane
Cover design by Mary Cartwright
Photography by Howard Allman

# Internet links

This book is a self-contained beginner's guide to drawing cartoons. You do not need a computer to enjoy it, but if you would like to find out more, there are brief descriptions of useful Web sites throughout the book. To visit these Web sites you need to go to the Usborne Quicklinks Web site at **www.usborne-quicklinks.com** and type in the key words 'drawing cartoons'. You will find direct links to Web sites, as well as pictures and templates for you to download.

## What you need

Most of the Web sites listed in this book can be accessed with a standard home computer and an Internet browser (the software that enables you to display information from the Internet). Here's a list of the basic requirements:
– A PC with Microsoft® Windows® 95 or later versions, or a Macintosh PowerPC with System 8.0 or later, and 64Mb RAM
– A browser such as Microsoft® Internet Explorer 4, or Netscape® Navigator 4, or later versions
– Connection to the Internet via a modem (preferably 56Kbps) or a faster digital or cable line
– An account with an Internet Service Provider (ISP)
– A sound card to hear sound files

## Extras

Some Web sites need additional programs, called plug-ins, to play sounds, or to show videos, animations or 3-D images. If you go to a site and you do not have the necessary plug-in, a message saying so will come up on the screen. There is usually a button on the site that you can click on to download the plug-in. Alternatively, go to www.usborne-quicklinks.com and click on Net Help. There you can find links to download plug-ins. Here is a list of plug-ins that you might need:
RealPlayer® – lets you play video and hear sound files
Quicktime – enables you to view video clips
Shockwave® – lets you play animations and interactive programs
Flash™ – lets you play animations

## Site availability

The links in Usborne Quicklinks are regularly reviewed and updated, but occasionally, you may get a message that a site is unavailable. This might be temporary, so try again later, or even the next day. If any of the recommended sites close down, we will, if possible, replace them with suitable alternatives, so you will always find up-to-date links to sites in Usborne Quicklinks.

## Downloadable pictures

Selected pictures, clip art and templates from this book can be downloaded from the Usborne Quicklinks Web site free of charge, for your own personal use.

The pictures must not be copied or distributed for any commercial or profit-related purpose. To find these pictures, go to the Usborne Quicklinks Web site and type in the key words 'drawing cartoons'.

★ Look out for this star symbol throughout the book. It marks pictures which you can download from the Usborne Quicklinks Web site.

## Internet safety

When using the Internet, make sure you follow these guidelines:
– Ask your parent's or guardian's permission before you log on to the Internet.
– If you write a message in a Web site guest book or on a Web site message board, do not include your e-mail address or any other personal information such as your real name, address or telephone number.
– If a Web site asks you to log in or register by typing your name or e-mail address, ask permission from an adult first.
– If you do receive e-mail from someone you don't know, tell an adult and do not reply to the e-mail.
– Never arrange to meet anyone you have talked to on the Internet.

All the sites described in this book have been selected by Usborne editors as suitable, in their opinion, for children, although no guarantees can be given and Usborne Publishing is not responsible for the accuracy or suitability of the information on any Web site other than its own. We recommend that young children are supervised while on the Internet and that children do not use Internet chat rooms.

## Computer viruses

A computer virus is a program that can seriously damage your computer. A virus can get into your computer when you download programs from the Internet, or in an attachment (an extra file) that arrives with an e-mail. You can buy anti-virus software at computer stores or download it from the Internet. It is quite expensive, but costs less than repairing a damaged computer. At www.usborne-quicklinks.com you'll find a link to the How Stuff Works Web site where you can find out more about computer viruses.

## Getting to the sites

To reach the Web sites described in this book, go to Usborne Quicklinks at **www.usborne-quicklinks.com** and type in the key words 'drawing cartoons'. Then, follow the instructions given there.

> ## A COMPUTER IS NOT ESSENTIAL TO USE THIS BOOK
> This guide to drawing cartoons is a complete, self-contained book.

# Contents

# Getting started

All you need to start drawing cartoons is a pencil and some paper. Look at cartoons on television, in comics and books, or on the Internet for inspiration. Here are some ideas of more things you can do to get started.

## Drawing and collecting

Cartoonists keep sketchbooks which they fill with lots of drawings, ideas and information. Keep a folder and fill it with sketches of cartoon ideas, postcards, comics and strips from newspapers.

Sketch people in different positions for future reference.

Keep a sketchbook of your cartoon ideas.

Buy comics for inspiration.

Collect comic strips printed in newspapers.

Collect postcards of famous cartoon characters.

Walt Disney's
**MICKEY MOUSE**
©Disney

## Ideas

As well as using pencil to draw cartoons, this book explains how to use other materials, too. It also contains lots of ideas for drawing different styles of cartoons.

Find out how to draw characters showing emotions on pages 30-31.

Find out how to make moving cartoons on page 50.

Find out how to draw superheroes on page 46.

★ Look out for this star symbol throughout the book. It marks pictures which you can download from the Usborne Quicklinks Web site.

Watch cartoons online, including *Scooby-Doo*, *Tom and Jerry*, *The Powerpuff Girls* and *Rugrats*, play games, or get some drawing tips. For links to these Web sites, go to **www.usborne-quicklinks.com** and type the key words 'drawing cartoons'.

# Expressions

An essential part of drawing cartoons is being able to draw expressions. You can draw lots of different expressions very simply. Then, you can use these to create complete cartoon characters.

Take an online lesson in how to draw some simple faces. Or, play a game online, adding parts to a potato to create funny faces. For a link to these Web sites, go to **www.usborne-quicklinks.com**

## A basic face

1. Draw a rough oval shape. It needn't be too neat. If it's lopsided it will add character.

2. Draw two small ovals for eyes, and put dots in them. Add a curve for a mouth.

## Changing expressions

Using just the eyes and mouth on a face, you can draw all sorts of expressions. Copy the faces on the fruit below and try combining different eyes and mouths to vary their expressions.

Grinning

Surprised

Sleepy

Sad

Laughing

Mischievous

Angry

Bashful

See page 59 for more expressions.

★

# Making a character

A basic circle face, with just a mouth and eyes, already has lots of personality. Without adding much more, you can make simple cartoon characters. For example, just add legs to make a spider, or add wings and legs to make a flying insect.

Find out more about how to show movement on pages 36-37.

In a cartoon garden, even the flowers can have faces.

# Different faces

A simple circle can make a person's face, but it's fun to vary the shape of faces you draw to give your cartoons different characters, like the ones you can see here. Experiment with drawing different hair, eyes, noses and mouths.

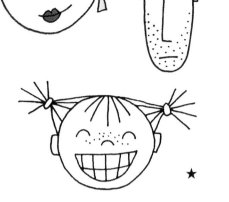

## Grinning girl

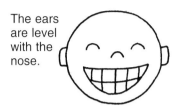

The ears are level with the nose.

1. Draw a circle for the head. Add little curves for the eyes and nose. Add a semicircle for a mouth.

2. Draw a line across the mouth. Add vertical lines for the teeth. Add ears halfway down each side.

3. Draw lines for pigtails on both sides of the head. Draw a few lines for a fringe. Add dots for freckles over the nose.

## Worried man

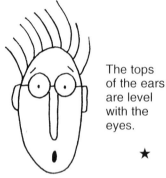

The tops of the ears are level with the eyes.

1. Draw a long oval for the head. Add circles with dots in them for eyes. Between the eyes, add a very long nose.

2. Add an oval mouth. Draw a line to join the circles around the eyes. Add lines to the sides of the head for glasses.

3. Draw two curves for ears. Add little lines for raised eyebrows. Add long lines for hair on top of the head.

All of these faces were drawn using black felt-tip pen. Then, some parts were added or filled in using coloured felt-tip pens.

# Angry baddie

Add little lines inside the ears.

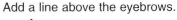

Add a line above the eyebrows.

1. Draw the head as a curved shape with a flat bottom. Add a line for the eyebrows. Then, add a rectangular nose.

2. Draw curves from the nose to the eyebrows, and add dots in them for eyes. Draw ears, level with the eyes.

3. Draw a big downward curve for a mouth. Add a smaller one beneath it. Add dots on the chin for stubble. Draw lines for hair.

# Cool lady

1. Draw an oval face. Add oval eyes, with a line across each one. Then, add pupils looking to one side.

2. Add a small nose. Draw an 'm'-shape and then underline it for the top lip. Add a curve for the bottom lip.

3. For the hair, draw a big curve from the top of the head. Join it to the face at the bottom. Do the same for the other side.

To create this crowd scene, the people at the front were drawn first, then the people further back.

As well as varying the people's faces, try varying the shapes of their bodies, and their clothes.

# Drawing bodies

In cartoons a character's body can be whatever shape you want it to be. Here are some tips for drawing cartoon people's bodies. You can vary the shapes to get different characters.

☞ Take step-by-step lessons online to learn how to draw some famous cartoon characters. For links to these Web sites, go to **www.usborne-quicklinks.com**

In the comic *Asterix*, the two main characters are completely different sizes.

©2002 LES ÉDITIONS ALBERT RENÉ / GOSCINNY-UDERZO

## Body proportions

Cartoonists can vary the body proportions of their characters to create different effects. For example, the bigger the head looks in proportion to the body, the cuter or more child-like the character will look.

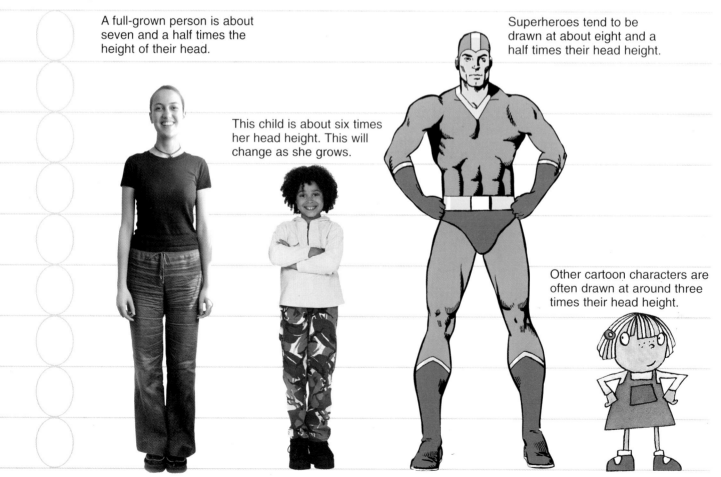

A full-grown person is about seven and a half times the height of their head.

This child is about six times her head height. This will change as she grows.

Superheroes tend to be drawn at about eight and a half times their head height.

Other cartoon characters are often drawn at around three times their head height.

# Body building

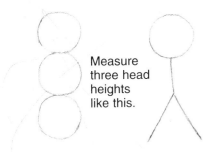

Measure three head heights like this.

1. In pencil, draw a circle for the head and then a line for the body. Add two stick legs coming from the body.

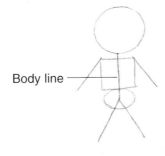

Body line

2. Add a rectangle for the ribs and an oval for the hips. The legs start halfway through the hip oval. Add stick arms.

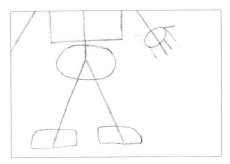

3. For the hands, draw ovals and add stick fingers and thumbs. Then, add feet to the bottoms of the stick legs.

4. Draw a face and hair using techniques and ideas given on pages 8 and 9. Add two lines for the neck.

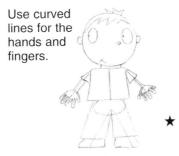

Use curved lines for the hands and fingers.

5. Draw a T-shirt and trousers. (See page 12 for more about clothing.) Then, outline the arms and the hands.

Add the details, like laces in the shoes, after rubbing out the pencil.

6. Go over the outline using a felt-tip pen. Leave it to dry, and then rub out all the pencil lines inside the figure.

Use the step-by-step instructions above, but vary how big you draw each part to get different body shapes.

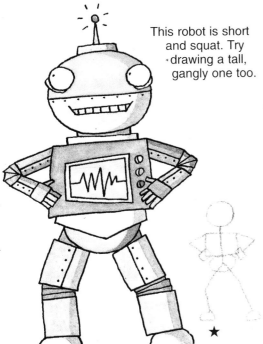

This robot is short and squat. Try drawing a tall, gangly one too.

To draw an older child, make the arms and legs longer.

A gorilla has very long arms and short legs.

11

# Cartoon clothes

Adding certain types of clothes to a cartoon character can help show who the character is. For instance, a cowboy hat, jeans, a neckerchief, and boots are often used to show a cowboy; a tall, puffy hat and white clothes are often used for a chef.

Chefs can have checked trousers, too.

Clowns usually have face paint and a red nose. They can also wear very big shoes.

© D. C. Thomson & Co., Ltd., 2001

This is Desperate Dan from the comic, *The Dandy*. He is a larger-than-life cowboy who always dresses in these clothes.

Cartoon burglars usually wear a striped top and an eye mask.

## Superhero family photo

Draw the faces next to each other.

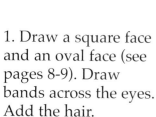

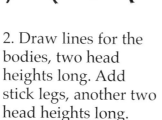

1. Draw a square face and an oval face (see pages 8-9). Draw bands across the eyes. Add the hair.

2. Draw lines for the bodies, two head heights long. Add stick legs, another two head heights long.

3. Add a triangle for the man's chest. Add an oval for his hips. Add a smaller triangle and oval to the woman.

4. Draw a girl's face and a boy's face in front. Add stick bodies with shapes on them (see page 11 for help).

5. For the outline, first draw the neck. Then, draw the arms as far as the wrists. Add the body up to the waist.

6. Next, draw the outline for the legs. Add oval feet on the ends. Then, draw hands on the hips.

7. Draw the cloak, adding 'v' shapes around the neck. Add lines for the edges of the boots and gloves.

8. Draw over your outline using felt-tip pen. Rub out all the pencil lines. You can then colour it in.

To draw more serious superheroes, use the proportions suggested on page 10, and follow the steps on page 46.

This picture was drawn using permanent felt-tip pen, and painted using watercolours (see pages 22-23).

# Cartoon creatures

Animals are lots of different shapes and sizes. However, you can use the same, simple shapes to draw all kinds of four-legged animals. All you have to do is vary the sizes of each part of the body.

Use these basic shapes to draw all kinds of four-legged creatures. You will need to add different snouts and tails for different animals.

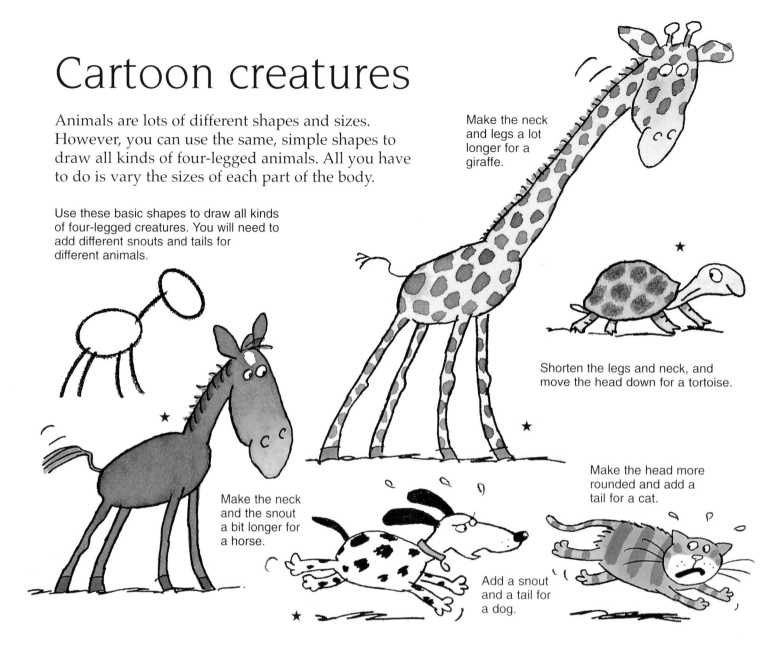

Make the neck and legs a lot longer for a giraffe.

Shorten the legs and neck, and move the head down for a tortoise.

Make the head more rounded and add a tail for a cat.

Make the neck and the snout a bit longer for a horse.

Add a snout and a tail for a dog.

# People and their pets

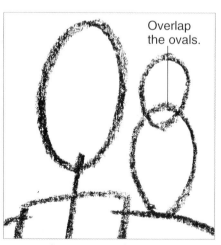

Overlap the ovals.

1. In pencil, draw shapes for a man's body using the steps on page 11. Don't add the face yet.

2. On the man's shoulder, draw an oval parrot's body with a head on top. The ovals should overlap a little.

3. Draw a big, curved beak on the parrot's face. Draw a big, beak-like nose on the man's face. Add the man's mouth.

★

Add some more detail in pen, such as buttons and a tie.

4. Add big, oval eyes on the man's face and on the parrot's. Add the pupils, leaving a little white dot in each for highlights.

5. Draw the parrot's feathers and the man's hair. Add the parrot's toes. Draw the man's suit. Add his hands and shoes.

6. Outline the two bodies in felt-tip pen. Let them dry, and then rub out the pencil lines. Then, you can colour them in.

Use the basic shapes for animals from page 14 and people from page 11 to draw more people and their pets. Make them look similar by drawing similar faces or hair. Here are some examples.

This scene was drawn in permanent felt-tip pen and painted using watercolours (see pages 22-23).

This woman's hair makes her look like her poodle. Her jumper looks like its fur, too.

This girl has a long face like her horse. Her hair looks like the horse's mane.

This man has fuzzy hair like his dog's ears. Their coats are similar too!

15

# Animal characters

You can give different animals of one kind, for example cats or dogs, personalities of their own. Vary their expressions and body shapes to create different characters.

In the cartoon *Duckula*, each character is a different kind of bird: the nurse is an enormous hen, the butler is a vulture and Count Duckula, of course, is a duck.

☞ Learn how to draw the famous cartoon character, Scooby-Doo, or other famous animal characters, such as Bugs Bunny. For links to these Web sites, go to **www.usborne-quicklinks.com**

©FremantleMedia Enterprises Ltd.

## Butch bulldog

1. Draw a circle for the face. Draw a line for the eyebrows and then add eyes. Add a nose, a mouth and pointed teeth.

2. Add curves from the mouth for jowls. Add the body. Then, add stick legs with oval paws, ears and a tail.

3. Outline the legs, tail and ears. Add a patch on its back. Add lines for the wagging tail and draw lines on the paws.

# Snooty pooch

1. Draw a bean-shaped head. Add eyes, a nose and a mouth. Draw a cloud shape for fur, and a line and fur for an ear.

2. Draw a long bean shape for the body and add a cloud shape at the bottom. Add stick legs with paws, and a stick tail.

3. Add more cloud shapes for fur around the neck, on the legs and on the end of the tail. Fill in the paws and the nose.

# Scruffy mongrel

Add little lines by the tail.

1. Draw an oval for the head. Add an oval snout. Add lines and ovals for ears on top. Add the nose and a tongue.

2. Draw a body. Add stick legs and a curved stick tail. Then, draw shaggy fur on the ears and over the eyes.

3. Add more shaggy fur on the rest of the body and the tail. Add some fur to the snout. Fill in the nose.

Draw the dogs in pencil, then use felt-tip pens to outline them and fill them in.

17

# Animal barn dance

Another way of drawing cartoon animals is to stand them up, give them clothes and make them more like people. You can draw the animals in human situations to add to the humour.

## Dippy giraffe girl

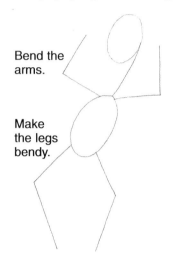

Bend the arms.

Make the legs bendy.

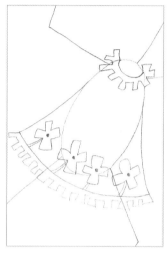

Add a line for the hoof.

1. In pencil, draw an oval head. Add a long stick neck. Draw a slanted oval body. Then, add long stick arms and legs.

2. Draw horns and ears on the head. Add eyes with lines for eyelids and lashes. Then, add the snout, mouth and nostrils.

3. For the dress, draw a curved neckline and then add the sides and bottom. Add frills along the edges. Draw a pattern on the dress.

4. Outline the long arms, legs and neck. Draw lines along the neck for a mane. Add high-heeled shoes to the feet.

## Honky-tonk horse

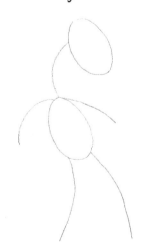

Make the neck quite thick.

The T-shirt is quite short.

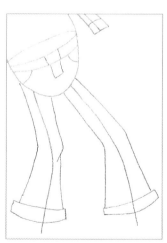

1. Draw an oval head. Add a curved stick neck and a long, oval body. Draw bendy stick legs and bendy arms.

2. Draw the ears and add the mouth. Draw oval eyes and nostrils. Then, outline the curved neck.

3. Draw a curved neckline. Add the rest of the T-shirt. Then, outline the bendy arms and add hooves.

4. Draw the waistband of the jeans and add a belt. Draw the rest of the jeans. Add pockets and a zip.

18

These animals were outlined in permanent felt-tip pen, and then painted using watercolours. (See page 22-23 for how to do this.)

A slogan was added to the horse's T-shirt.

I ♥ HAY

Dashes show the stitching on the jeans.

These hens have aprons on and are using their feathered wings as hands.

Spur

5. Add some cowboy boots. Draw heels and spurs on them. Then, add lines for the mane and tail.

You can make animals' paws into three-fingered hands, like this rabbit's.

19

# Inking and shading

Most cartoonists draw cartoons in pencil first. Then, when they are sure the cartoon is correct, they outline it and fill in the dark areas with black. This is called inking. Here are some ideas for inking cartoons to get different effects.

Many comic strips that appear in newspapers, such as this *Garfield* strip by Jim Davis, are printed only in black and white.

## Light and dark

You can bring cartoons to life and make them look solid by inking them to show light and dark areas. When light shines on something, the parts nearest the light are the palest and the parts furthest from the light are the darkest.

The light on this teapot is shining from this side.

Cartoonists often simplify shading into light and dark without using any medium shades.

Cartoons often use a window-shaped highlight on shiny surfaces, even if there isn't a window in the scene.

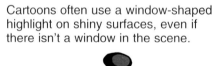

1. Draw the outline of the teapot above in pencil. Look at which parts are darkest. Outline them in pencil.

2. Go over the outline in pen. Then, fill in the darkest areas in pen. Let it dry, and then rub out all the pencil lines.

3. The teapot is very shiny, so look at where the light hits it. Draw a little curved window shape there for a highlight.

# Shadows

The size and shape of a shadow depends on where the light is coming from. A shadow always falls in the opposite direction from the source of light.

☞ Look at more *Garfield* comic strips online. Learn more about how to shade, too. For links to these Web sites, go to **www.usborne-quicklinks.com**

★

In the morning, when the sun is low in the sky, people throw long shadows along the ground.

In the middle of the day, the sun is directly overhead, so people throw short shadows.

At the end of the day, the sun sinks again. People throw shadows in the opposite direction from in the morning.

# Dramatic lighting

You can use dramatic lighting to give a scene atmosphere. You can also use light and dark areas to make the reader look at a particular area of the cartoon. Here are some examples.

The two faces in this cartoon stand out because they are much lighter than the rest of the scene.

Silhouettes against a bright background can be used to show an evening scene.

A big shadow, like the one below, can look threatening or funny.

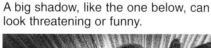

A shadowy face in a cartoon can look mysterious or threatening.

21

# Cartoon colour

Many cartoons have bright, bold colours. You can achieve these using felt-tip pens. However, many cartoonists use watercolour paints to add colour and shading. Here are some tips on using watercolours.

## Pen outline

To create a watercolour cartoon with a black outline, you need to use a permanent black felt-tip (one which doesn't blur when it gets wet). Before painting, draw the outline in permanent pen, then rub out any pencil lines.

Using your pencil line as a guide, draw the outline in permanent pen. Let it dry, then rub the pencil out.

If you only have a water-soluble felt-tip pen (one which blurs when it gets wet), then paint the cartoon first, and add the outline when the paint is dry.

## Watercolour paints

Watercolour paints come in tubes, or blocks called pans. To use pans, rub a wet paintbrush on the pan to get paint on the bristles. Then, dab the paint onto a saucer.

Add more water to get a paler colour. For white areas, just leave a gap so the paper shows.

Leave a colour to dry before painting another near it if you don't want them to blur.

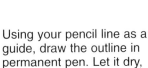

Watercolour pan

Watercolour tube paint

To use tubes, squeeze a little blob of paint onto a saucer. Dab a little water onto it with a paintbrush and mix it in.

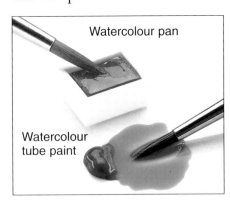

Paint the lightest parts first and then the darker parts.

Wet watercolours blur into one another. You can use this for special effects.

# Mixing colours

One advantage of using paint is that you can mix your own colours. There are three colours from which all other colours are made – red, yellow and blue. These are called the primary colours.

Mix yellow and blue to make green. Add more yellow or more blue to make different shades.

Mix red and yellow to make orange. Add more red or more yellow to make different shades.

Mix blue and red to make purple. Add more blue or more red to make different shades.

Mix red, yellow and blue together to make brown. To make different shades, alter how much you use of each colour.

To make a colour darker, add blue or brown. Try to avoid adding black, as it makes colours duller.

Green can be made darker by adding more blue. It can be made lighter by adding yellow.

# Painting scenes

There are different ways of painting backgrounds using watercolours. These pages show two ways of painting backgrounds, and also watercolour techniques you can use to make a funny cartoon monster scene.

## Painting backgrounds

1. Draw the whole cartoon, including the background, in permanent pen.

2. Paint clean water over the background. This will help you to get an even colour.

3. On the damp paper, paint the background. Paint pale colours before the darker ones.

4. When the background is completely dry, fill in the foreground, or the main characters.

## Monster moon scene

1. Dampen your paper by painting water onto it or by wiping a damp sponge on it.

2. While it is still damp, mix lots of a very pale colour. Paint it on with a large brush.

3. While the paper is damp, mix a slightly darker shade and paint it on. The colours will blur together.

4. When the background is dry, mix a bright colour and paint a blob. It doesn't matter what shape it is.

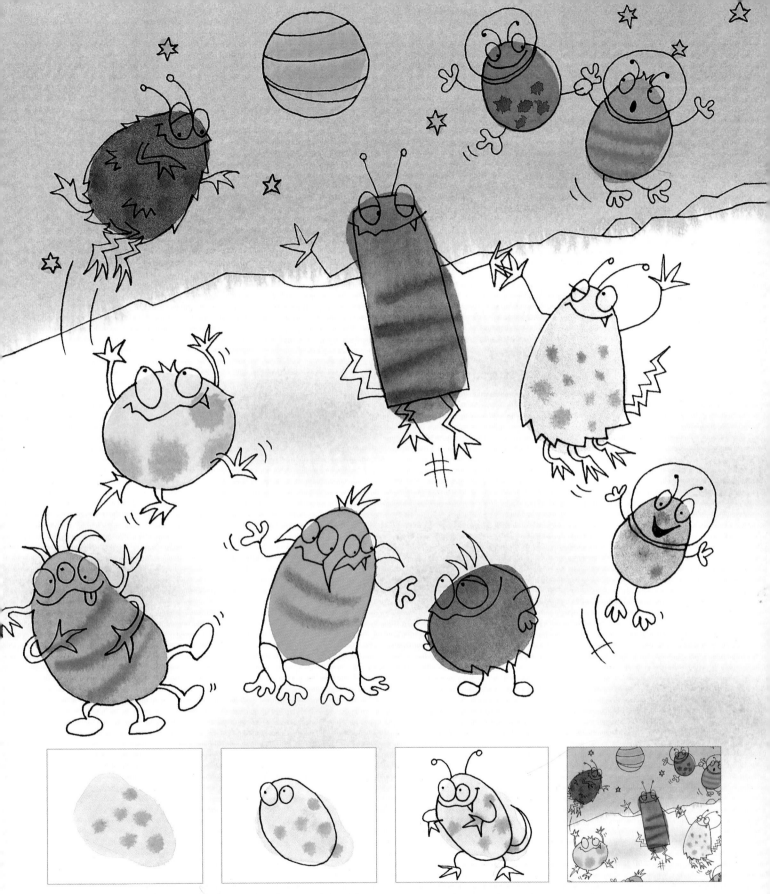

5. While the blob is damp, add little dots of another colour. They will blur on the damp paper.

6. When it is dry, draw some eyes at the top. Add an outline. It doesn't have to follow the coloured shape.

7. Add some antennae. Then draw some arms and legs. You can add a tail and other details, such as fangs.

8. Add more monsters to the scene following steps 4 to 7. Outline the planet and the rest of the background last.

# Colour effects

By using particular combinations of colours in a cartoon, you can create special effects. For example, you can use blues and greens ('cool' colours) to show a cold scene, and reds, oranges and yellows ('warm' colours) to show a hot scene.

A rising sun might make the whole sky yellow and throw warm-looking light across a scene.

A snowy scene can be shown by using white with icy blue shadows.

A night scene can be shown using blue with yellow highlights.

# In the spotlight

1. Draw a shape for the body. Add a head. Draw eyes, a mouth, ears and a nose. Then, add stick arms and legs.

2. Draw a top hat and a cane at the ends of the stick arms. Then, draw the arms and legs. Add the bristles.

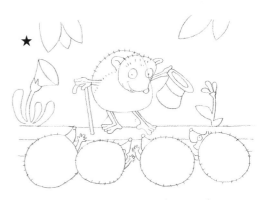

3. Draw some more hedgehogs as an audience. Then, add a wall. Draw some plants and leaves around it.

4. Draw the outline in permanent pen and rub out the pencil lines. Then, paint the yellow areas shown here.

5. Let it dry. Paint the blue areas. Then, mix shades of brown (see page 23) and paint the hedgehogs and the wall.

6. When it is dry, paint the plants in different shades of green and blue. Paint the hat and cane red.

# Moving bodies

To draw a cartoon character from different angles you have to make it look three-dimensional. To do this, you can draw construction lines in pencil to help you get everything in the right place. You can rub these out when the drawing is finished.

Look at some drawings of famous characters from different angles. Also, take some online lessons on drawing faces and bodies in different positions. For links to these sites, go to www.usborne-quicklinks.com

## Turning faces

Construction lines drawn on an orange can help you to see how the eyes, nose and mouth move when a face moves into different positions. The facial features always stay in the same position in relation to where the lines cross.

You can use these photos of a face on an orange as reference for how to draw a face in different positions.

Facing the front, the construction lines look straight.

Draw a circle. Add two construction lines making a cross inside. Then add the eyes, nose, mouth and ears.

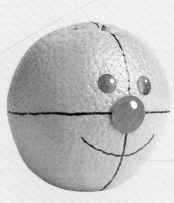

Looking to the side, the vertical line looks curved.

Draw a circle. Add the construction lines, making the vertical line curve to one side. Then, add the face.

Looking down, the horizontal line looks curved.

Draw a circle. Add the construction lines, making the horizontal line bend downward. Then, add the face.

Looking upward, the horizontal line looks curved.

Draw a circle. Add the construction lines, making the horizontal line bend upward. Add the face.

Looking down and to the side, both lines look curved.

Draw a circle. Add the construction lines, making both the horizontal and the vertical lines bend. Then, add the face.

# Turning bodies

To draw a body from different angles, you can use similar techniques to those used for the head. Here are some tips.

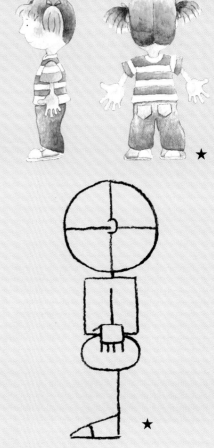

Use the shapes on page 11 to draw a body from the front. To draw shoes from the front, draw a triangle and then add a semicircle for the toe.

To draw someone turning slightly, draw a slanted square for the body. Add arms to the top corners. Draw triangle shapes for the feet.

From the side, one arm moves to the middle of the body shape, in line with the spine. The nearest leg completely overlaps the one further away.

From the back, the body shapes look similar to those from the front. But only the backs of the ears show, and the feet are triangles without the toe shapes.

## Focus on hands and feet

Cartoon hands and feet can have any number of fingers or toes. Many cartoon hands use only three fingers. You can adjust the following examples to fit any number of fingers or toes.

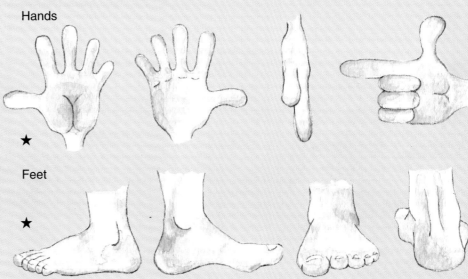

Hands

Feet

# Body language

You can add comedy to cartoon characters by using body language to tell part of the story. This means drawing the characters in positions which show what they are feeling or doing. Cartoons tend to use very exaggerated poses.

©Disney

This man is reaching down with his arms and his legs are flying into the air with the effort of swatting at the fly.

In this picture, Donald Duck's fists are clenched and his brow is furrowed. His whole body position shows that he is furious.

A character might jump into another character's arms out of fright!

Someone reluctant to go somewhere might lean back.

Someone eager to go fast might lean foward as they run.

Someone waving their hands in the air and jumping can look overjoyed.

An unhappy character might look down and put their hands in their pockets.

# A fatal attraction

Sometimes you can set a scene or tell a cartoon joke just using body language. The scenery can help add to the humour.

Add whiskers on each side.

Make the girl cat's eyes wide and add eyelashes.

Outline their heads before their bodies.

1. For a cat's face, draw an oval with a curve inside. Add eyes, a nose and a mouth. Add furry cheeks and ears.

2. Draw a girl cat's head, as shown here. Then, add oval bodies with stick legs and long tails. Add the feet.

3. Draw their clothes. Add shoes and other details. Then, outline them in permanent pen and rub out the pencil lines.

This scene was drawn in permanent felt-tip pen and then painted using watercolours.

The cats were drawn first and then the background was added.

A bird and some clouds were added here to show how high the drop off the cliff might be.

The worm looking over the edge shows how high the cliff is.

# Comic strips

In comic strips, cartoonists draw boxes known as frames around each picture in the strip. Each frame shows a moment in time. Normally when you look at a comic strip you 'read' the frames from left to right, and from the top to the bottom of the page.

☞ Look at more *Peanuts* comic strips and watch some cartoon clips. Look at other famous comic strips online, too, for inspiration. For links to these Web sites, go to **www.usborne-quicklinks.com**

  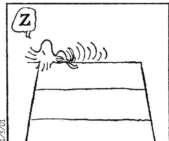 

This *Peanuts* strip by Charles Schulz is a good example of a simple use of cartoon frames to tell a little story.

## Framing the story

There are lots of ways in which you can use frames in a comic strip. Here are some examples and tips on how to create a comic strip.

You can vary the size of the frames to make the strip more interesting or to make a point.

You can zoom right in on a character to make an impact.

Make a character break out of the frame for a dramatic effect.

Before you start drawing the comic strip, make some rough sketches to work out how many frames you want to use.

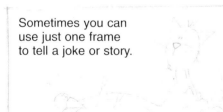

Sometimes you can use just one frame to tell a joke or story.

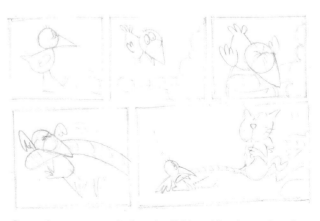

Sometimes a story is funnier if it's told using a few frames.

# Mistaken identity

Before drawing the final comic strip, make sketches of the characters you want to use, to work out how they will look. To draw the comic strip below, first draw out the frames on the paper. Then, draw inside each frame using pencil.

To draw the crow in different positions, just alter the positions of the shapes.

1. Draw a circle for a head. Add a triangular beak and a grin. Then, draw the eyes and tufts for feathers on the head.

2. Draw a semicircle for a body. Draw a wing and some tail feathers. Add stick legs and feet.

Add some whiskers, too.

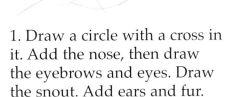

1. Draw a circle with a cross in it. Add the nose, then draw the eyebrows and eyes. Draw the snout. Add ears and fur.

2. Draw a big teardrop shape for the body. Add a long tail. Then, add stick legs and stick arms. Draw triangular paws.

3. Outline the arms – one overlapping the other. Outline the legs and feet, too, and add fingers to the paws.

This comic strip was drawn in permanent felt-tip pen and then painted using watercolours.

You don't need to use a ruler for drawing frames – these were drawn by hand.

# Speaking and thinking

You can add words to single cartoons or comic strips, to make the characters speak, think or yelp, for example, or just to tell the reader what's going on.

☞ Get tips on doing lettering in cartoons. Also, you can look at styles of lettering (fonts) for ideas, or download fonts to use on your computer. For links to these sites, go to **www.usborne-quicklinks.com**

## Speech bubbles

In comics, there are ways to draw speech bubbles so that the reader knows whether a character is actually talking, thinking, shouting or whispering. If you like, you can use pictures instead of words inside thought bubbles.

A cloud-shaped bubble like this contains thoughts or dreams.

This is a speech bubble. The tail should point towards the speaker.

The jagged edges on this speech bubble show that the character is shouting.

A speech bubble with dashes instead of edges contains a whisper.

## Drawing bubbles

When you add a speech bubble, draw it in pencil first, just in case your words don't fit and you need to make it bigger. When choosing where to position the bubbles in a strip, remember that you read comics from left to right and from top to bottom.

1. Draw ovals for the speech bubbles using pencil. Then, add little, curved tails pointing towards each speaker.

2. Draw straight lines in the bubble and then write the text along them. Don't worry about fitting it all inside the bubble.

3. Go over the text in pen. If you need to, redraw the speech bubble so it fits around the words. Outline it in pen.

34

## Speaking in character

You can use different styles of writing to show different characters' voices. Big letters show a loud voice and small letters show a quiet one.

## Speechless

There are other ways of expressing a character's thoughts or reactions without using speech. Comics and cartoons use particular symbols to show certain things. Here are some examples.

ZZZ shows that a character is asleep or snoring.

A light bulb appearing over someone's head means they've had an idea.

An exclamation mark above someone's head shows their shock or surprise.

A question mark above a character's head shows their confusion.

Hearts can show someone's fallen in love. They can have hearts in their eyes, too.

If someone is hit on the head, flying stars and birds show that they are dazed.

# Chasing and racing

There are tricks cartoonists use to show things moving in their drawings. Motion lines are the most common technique, but you can also add puffs of dust and words, or use a blurring effect to show movement.

☞ Take a look at characters and vehicles from the cartoon *Wacky Races* to get inspiration for inventing more racing vehicles. Watch a clip from the cartoon. For links to these sites, go to **www.usborne-quicklinks.com**

## Zooming car

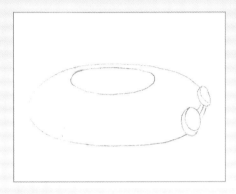

These are motion lines.

1. Draw an oval car body. Add another oval for the opening in the top. Draw headlights and a grill at the front.

2. Add slanted oval wheels. Add a character inside the car, leaning forward, and holding a wheel. Add the bumpers.

3. Drawing quickly, add two downward strokes behind the car and by each wheel. Draw horizontal lines from the back.

This race was outlined in pen and then painted using watercolours. The techniques described above were used to show the speed of all the racers.

A number was added to each racer, so they look like they are in an official race.

# Blurred legs

1. Draw an oval head with long ears. Add a stick body leaning forward. Draw an oval on it. Add an arm and a tail.

2. Draw a scribbly oval where the legs would normally go. The legs are moving so fast they look like a blur.

3. Drawing quickly, add some motion lines at the bottom of the blurred legs. Then, add some little puffs of dust.

# Sound effects

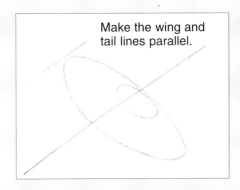

Make the wing and tail lines parallel.

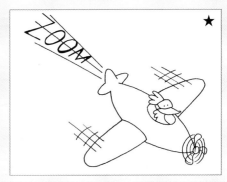

1. Draw an oval body for the plane. Add an oval cockpit. Pressing lightly, add diagonal lines for the wings and tail.

2. Outline the wings and tail. Add a character inside the cockpit. Add the propeller with scribbly circles on it.

3. Draw lines from the back of the plane. Then write 'zoom' inside the lines. Add motion lines behind the wings.

# Stretching and squashing

In cartoons, characters and objects can be stretched or squashed to create various special effects. Cartoonists use squashing and stretching to show speed, weight or impact (something hitting something else).

A cartoon ball bouncing along squashes when it hits the floor and stretches when it lifts off again.

The speed at which this centipede is running is shown by all the slanted ovals.

The centipede is going so fast it isn't even touching the ground.

> Take online tutorials to learn more about how to draw things stretching and squashing in cartoons. For links to these sites, go to **www.usborne-quicklinks.com**

As the centipede hits a wall, its whole body squashes up.

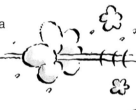

## Banana slip-up

The following step-by-steps show you how to draw the baby elephant from the comic strip on the next page.

Add a shadow beneath the elephant.

1. Draw an oval head. Add an oval body. Add big eyes and a long, curved trunk. Then, add stick arms and legs.

2. Put dots in the eyes. Add ears and a tail. Draw ovals on the ends of the legs and arms. Then, draw their outlines.

3. Draw the elephant's outline, adding toenails and other details. Draw a banana skin. Then, add some motion lines.

Make the head and the body ovals overlap.

Use a wavy line for the trunk.

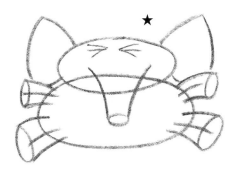

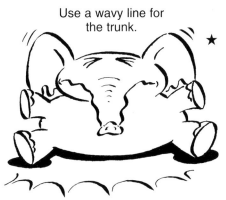

1. Draw a squashed oval head with a squashed oval body. Draw the eyes shut tight. Add stick arms and legs.

2. Draw a short trunk. Add triangular ears. Draw ovals on the ends of the arms and legs. Then, draw their outlines.

3. Add the toenails. Draw the elephant's outline. Fill in a shadow underneath. Then, add curved lines to show the impact.

This comic strip was drawn with permanent pen and painted with watercolours.

39

# Cartoon antics

In the world of cartoons, anything can happen. Characters can fall off cliffs, or they can be flattened or stretched into all sorts of extraordinary shapes but be unhurt. Here are a few classic cartoon antics, to give you some ideas.

## Dynamite

Cartoon dynamite doesn't actually hurt the characters. It just makes them turn black and sooty for a short while.

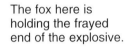
The fox here is holding the frayed end of the explosive.

## Running off cliffs

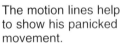
The motion lines help to show his panicked movement.

If a cartoon character runs off a cliff, they will stay hanging in mid air until they notice there's no ground beneath them. Then, they will plummet to the ground very, very quickly.

## Brick wall

If a character in a cartoon runs fast enough, they can go straight through a brick wall. They leave a hole shaped exactly like them behind.

## Steamroller

If a character is rolled over by a steamroller, they will be flattened like a pancake and become taller than they were before. But, moments later they will spring back to their normal shape.

The moons and stars show that he's a little dazed.

# Harebrained scheme

In lots of famous cartoons, one animal always chases after another, inventing more and more harebrained schemes to try to catch them. They never succeed. Here's how to draw a fox planning a mad invention to catch a chicken.

Watch some antics of famous characters, such as Wile E. Coyote and Road Runner or Tom and Jerry, online. For links to these sites, go to **www.usborne-quicklinks.com**

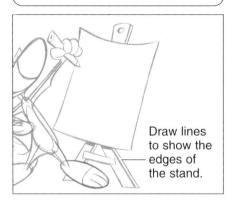

Draw lines to show the edges of the stand.

1. Draw a semicircle for a head. Add a snout, eyes and a mouth. Then, draw the body. Add stick legs and arms with oval paws.

2. Add ears, eyebrows and a tail. Draw a pencil, then add fingers on one paw. Then, draw the rest of the arms and legs.

3. For the easel, draw a rough rectangle for the board. Add the stand at the top and add the legs.

You could also use chalk or white pencil for drawing the plan.

4. Draw the 'plan' shown here on the board. Outline the scene in permanent pen, but leave the plan in pencil.

5. Colour the scene using felt-tip pens or watercolours. Let it dry. Then, use correction fluid to go over the plan lines.

# Perspective

The further away things are from you the smaller they look. This is called perspective. There are tricks you can use to show perspective in your cartoons to make them look three-dimensional.

In this cartoon, the path gets smaller and smaller into the distance until you can't see it any more. The point at which it disappears from view is called the vanishing point.

Horses and a cowboy were added to make a Western street scene.

This is the vanishing point.

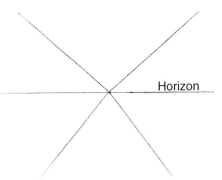

1. Draw a horizontal line for the horizon. Then, add four slanted lines coming from one point on the horizon.

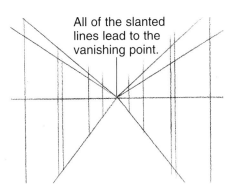

All of the slanted lines lead to the vanishing point.

2. Add vertical lines for the walls of each building. Add more slanted lines for the tops of the buildings.

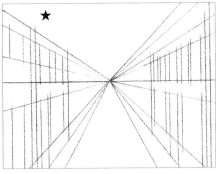

3. For the windows and doors, draw more slanted lines from the vanishing point. Then, add vertical lines for their sides.

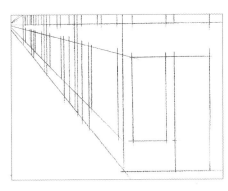

4. Draw horizontal lines for the fronts of the buildings on the street facing you. Add windows and doors.

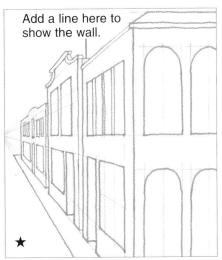

Add a line here to show the wall.

5. Add a pavement line and roofs to the buildings. Shape the doors, windows and fronts of the buildings.

6. Add frames around the windows and doors. You can add details, such as awnings on shop fronts and tiles on roofs.

43

# Skewed views

If you want to show something from a character's point of view, you can warp the drawing so that it looks like you are seeing it from a certain angle. This is another way of showing perspective (see page 42).

(see page 42).

Take a lesson to learn more about drawing using perspective, or look at a Web site for ideas on drawing from a character's point of view. For links to these Web sites, go to **www.usborne-quicklinks.com**

## Worm's eye view

If you were very small and you looked up at a very tall person, such as this giant, his body would seem to get smaller and smaller the further away from you it became.

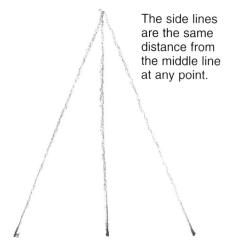

The side lines are the same distance from the middle line at any point.

1. Using pencil, draw a vertical line. Then, draw two diagonal lines coming from the same point at the top.

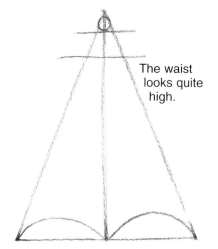

The waist looks quite high.

2. Draw two semicircles at the bottom. Then, mark a line for the waist and shoulders. Draw in a small circle for the head.

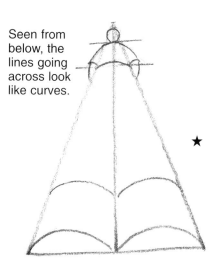

Seen from below, the lines going across look like curves.

3. Add the arms, and draw the shirt sleeves. Draw the curved waist line and shoulder line. Add curved trouser bottoms.

The eyes, nose and mouth are different shapes from underneath.

4. Draw eyes high on the head. Add the nose. Draw a mouth and add ears level with it. Add hairs on the chin and the head.

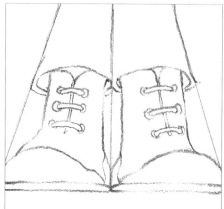

Finish off the bottoms of the trousers.

5. Add lines to show the soles of the shoes. Draw the sides of the boots. Add laces across and then draw the eyelets.

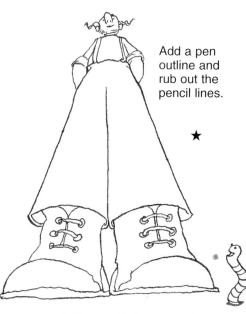

Add a pen outline and rub out the pencil lines.

Add a small character whose viewpoint you are sharing.

# Bird's eye view

If you could look down on a giant from above his head, his body would seem to get smaller and smaller, the further away from you it became.

The guidelines for drawing a person from a bird's eye view are the opposite way around from those for drawing a worm's eye view.

Mark where the shoulders and waist go before drawing the body.

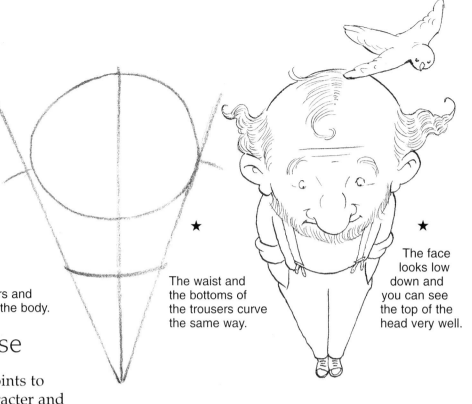

★

The waist and the bottoms of the trousers curve the same way.

★

The face looks low down and you can see the top of the head very well.

## A giant and a mouse

You can use these two viewpoints to alternate between a short character and a tall character in a comic strip.

Excuse me!

Excuse me!

You're standing on my tail!

Oh! I'm sorry little friend.

Wow! The world looks small from up here!

# Superheroes

Superheroes have special powers, which can be anything from superhuman strength, to being able to fly or change their shape. They are normally seen battling villains. These pages give you a starting point for drawing superheroes of your own, which you can use in scenes with the villains on pages 48-49.

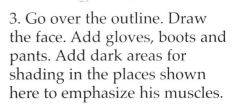

## Drawing a superhero

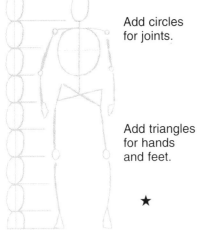

Add circles for joints.

Add triangles for hands and feet.

Draw a cross on the head before adding the face.

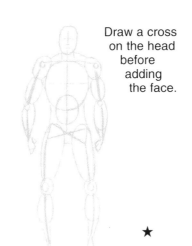

Draw lines on the face for cheek bones.

1. Draw an oval head and a stick body. Add an oval chest. Draw the hips, arms and legs. Make the figure eight and a half times its head height.

2. Add ovals for bulging muscles to the arms and legs. Add an oval for the stomach muscles. Outline the shoulders and waist.

3. Go over the outline. Draw the face. Add gloves, boots and pants. Add dark areas for shading in the places shown here to emphasize his muscles.

## Poses

The secret to making superheroes look dramatic and exciting, is to draw them in very exaggerated poses. The stick men below show some action poses you could use.

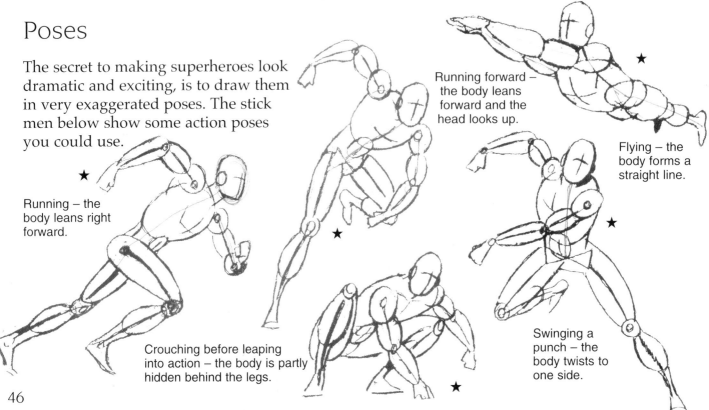

Running – the body leans right forward.

Running forward – the body leans forward and the head looks up.

Flying – the body forms a straight line.

Crouching before leaping into action – the body is partly hidden behind the legs.

Swinging a punch – the body twists to one side.

Watch a funny, interactive cartoon about superheroes with super-powerful chins! Read comics online, or look at famous superheroes for inspiration. For links to these sites, go to **www.usborne-quicklinks.com**

See page 49 for how to draw this villain.

# Villains

Baddies in action cartoons can be anything from evil scientists, to power-hungry businessmen or enormous swamp monsters. Here are some ideas for drawing villains.

☞ Look at some online galleries of famous villains for inspiration. For links to these Web sites, go to **www.usborne-quicklinks.com**

## Evil scientist

An evil scientist has a skinny, hunched body. He is an old man wearing a lab coat.

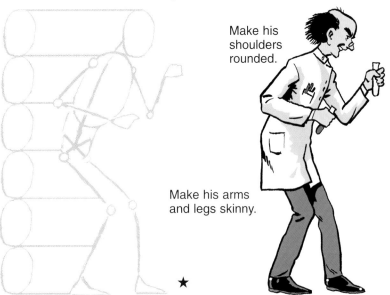

Make his shoulders rounded.

Make his arms and legs skinny.

★

Draw the hunched figure six heads high.

Add a test tube and a lab coat to show he is a scientist.

★

A sneaky scientist might look over his shoulder like this.

A scientist might grin, forming an evil plan.

A cowardly villain might gasp with fear.

## Power-hungry businessman

The power-hungry businessman has a squat body. He is middle-aged and wears a pin-striped suit.

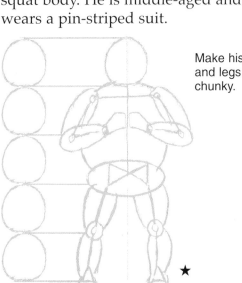

Make his arms and legs chunky.

A greedy villain might fling his arms out when saying he wanted to take over the world!

★

★

Draw the figure five heads high.

Add big, square-shaped hands.

An evil villain might laugh in triumph.

An evil villain might scowl with fury.

# Swamp monster

Monsters can take any shape you like. This swamp monster has a bulky, muscular body. Its head sinks low into its shoulders. It is covered in slime.

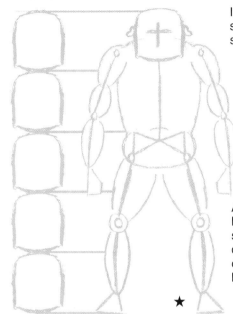

Draw the figure five heads high.

Its head is square-shaped.

Add wavy lines for slime dripping off its body.

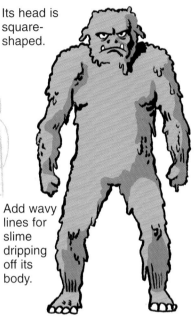

Add big toenails on the feet.

Getting hit – the body bends right back.

A confused monster might look like this.

A defeated monster might look like this.

To draw the villains in a scene, draw them in pencil first and then add the background.

# Animation

Moving cartoons, or animations, are made by showing still pictures very quickly one after the other. They are shown so quickly that your eye is fooled into thinking it sees a moving picture. To make a film, animators have to create every single picture that will be shown.

This is a still picture from the cartoon *Popeye*. It shows Olive Oyl and Popeye dancing.

©King Features Syndicate

## Flick book

To make a flick book you need a pad of paper which is thin enough to see through slightly. By drawing the same character over and over again, but changing its position a little each time, you can make it look as if it is moving.

★ Instead of drawing these frogs you can download them to make a flick book. To do this, go to **www.usborne-quicklinks.com**

1. Using quite dark pencil or felt-tip pen, draw a character on the back page of the pad in the bottom, right-hand corner.

2. Flip the next page on top and draw the character again, but in a slightly different position from the first time.

3. Flip to the next page. Draw the character on this page again, moving its position a little more.

4. Flip the next page on top. Draw the character again, remembering to only change the position slightly each time.

5. Continue flipping the pages over and drawing the character in a slightly different position on each of the pages.

6. Flick through the pages from the back of the pad to the front. The character will seem to be moving.

# Stages of animation

An animation has to go through lots of stages before becoming a finished cartoon. The pictures below show the different stages one drawing would go through before becoming a part of an animation.

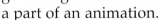

The final outline is drawn in black.

Next, the bird is drawn in blue pencil to get the position perfect.

First of all, 'roughs' are drawn to work out the character.

The finished cartoon is coloured in.

# Making a storyboard

Before making an animation, an animator will sketch out a story to show what happens. This is called making a storyboard. A storyboard looks like a comic strip, showing only the main actions. To make a storyboard, think of a story and then sketch it out in frames.

Find out how *Popeye* was first made as an animation. Take a tour at a famous animation studio. Alternatively, look at some storyboards of famous cartoons. You can watch animations or even create your own animation online. For links to all of these Web sites, go to **www.usborne-quicklinks.com**

You can use a storyboard to plan out a much longer animation than one you can make in a flick book.

Sound effects (SFX) for the actual cartoon are suggested in writing below the frames.

SFX- GUNSHOT

HA HA!

CRASH!! OOF!!

TWEET TWEET

CLICK

51

# Computer drawing

Many modern cartoons are drawn on computer. If you have a computer with Microsoft® Windows® on it, it will have a program called Paint, which you can use for drawing cartoons. Usually, you can open the program by following the steps below.

## Opening Paint

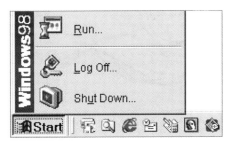

1. Using your mouse, position the pointer over the *Start* button and click (using the left mouse button). A list will pop up on your screen.

2. Move your pointer over the word *Programs*. Another list will appear. Move the pointer to *Accessories*. On the list that appears, click on *Paint*.

3. A box, or window, will appear. The white area in the middle is a page which you can draw on. There are tools for drawing around the edge.

## Paint tools

To draw you first need to choose a tool. To do this, position your pointer over a tool in the tool box and click on it. You may see options below the tool box, which you can click on, too. To choose a colour, click on a coloured square in the paint box.

This is the tool box.

If you click on the brush tool in the tool box, these options appear beneath. Click on one to choose a style and size of brush to use.

This is the paint box.

The colour you have chosen appears here.

To choose a colour to use, click on a coloured box.

## Drawing freehand

Click on the brush tool. Move the pointer to the page. Pressing the left mouse button down, drag the mouse to draw.

## Filling in

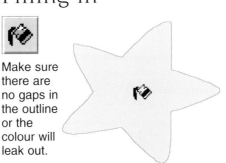

Make sure there are no gaps in the outline or the colour will leak out.

Click on the paint can. Click on a colour. Move the pointer over a shape and click to fill the shape with colour.

## Erasing

Click on the eraser. Pressing the left mouse button down, drag the pointer over whatever you want to rub out.

This scene was created using the tools described on these pages.

The spines on this puffer fish were drawn using the odd shape tool.

Select the brush tool and click to make dots in the eyes.

See page 56 for how to undo any mistakes you make.

## Drawing ovals

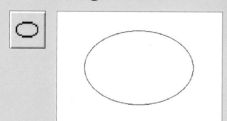

Click on the oval tool. Move the pointer over the page. Pressing the left mouse button, drag the mouse to draw an oval. Let go of the mouse button to finish the shape.

## Odd shapes

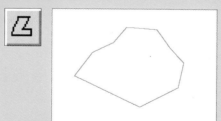

Click on the odd shape tool. Pressing the left mouse button, drag the mouse to draw a side. Let the button go, then press and drag to make another side. Double-click to finish the shape.

## Shape options

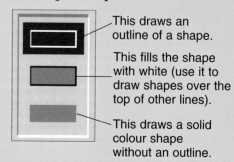

This draws an outline of a shape.

This fills the shape with white (use it to draw shapes over the top of other lines).

This draws a solid colour shape without an outline.

When you click on a shape tool, these three options appear beneath the tool box. Click on one to choose it.

# Computer cartoons

You can add words to pictures in Microsoft® Paint. You can use this to add speech bubbles to computer cartoons. These pages show you how to draw a cartoon with a speech bubble. Look at pages 52-53 if you need reminding how to use some of the tools.

## Draw a tortoise

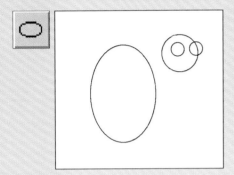

1. Click on the oval tool. Then, pressing the left mouse button, drag the pointer to draw a body, a head and two eyes.

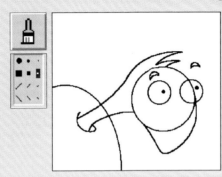

2. Click on the brush tool. Click on a small brush style option. Draw the neck and nose. Add eyebrows and dots in the eyes.

Add toenails on the feet.

3. Draw the edge of the tortoise's shell and then add lines on its body. Add arms, legs and a tail.

Check there are no gaps in the outline before you fill it in.

4. Click on the eraser. Rub out any extra lines. Click on the paint can and click on a colour. Click on the tortoise to fill it in.

If you make a mistake while drawing this, see page 56 for how to undo it.

# Add a speech bubble

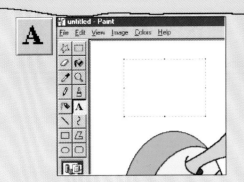

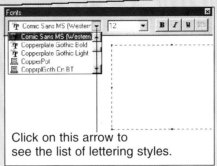

Click on this arrow to see the list of lettering styles.

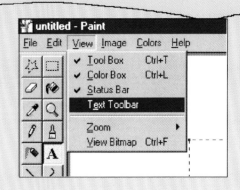

1. To add words, first click on the A tool. Pressing the left mouse button, drag the mouse to make a dotted box.

2. A 'Fonts' box will appear. It allows you to choose how the lettering will look. Click on the arrow to see a list.

3. If the Fonts box doesn't appear, click on *View* at the top of the window. On the list that appears, click on *Text Toolbar*.

These words were written using a lettering style called Comic Sans MS.

These words were written using size 10.

The dotted box around the words will disappear.

4. Click on an option in the list to choose a style of lettering. Then click in the dotted box. Type some words.

5. To change the letter size, click on the number in the Fonts box. Type a lower or higher number, then click inside the dotted box.

6. Click outside the dotted box to finish your lettering. It will become part of the picture, so you can't change it any more.

Use the eraser to rub out this line.

7. Click on the oval tool and on the top option that appears below the tool box. Draw an oval around the words.

8. Click on the brush. Click on a small brush style option below the tool box. Add a tail to the oval. Rub out the extra line.

# Computer comic strips

An advantage of using a computer to draw a comic strip is that there are tools you can use to copy a character, so it can appear again without you having to redraw it. Here are some tips for drawing a comic strip on computer.

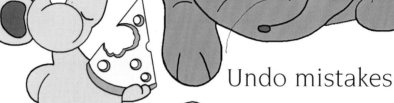

## Drawing frames

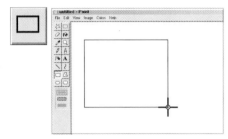

Click on the rectangle tool. Pressing the left mouse button down, drag the mouse to draw a rectangular frame.

## Undo mistakes

If you make a mistake, hold CTRL down on your keyboard and press the Z key. This deletes the last thing you did.

## Draw a mouse

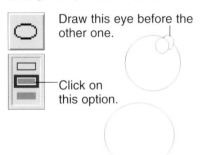

Draw this eye before the other one.

Click on this option.

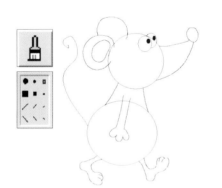

Make sure there are no gaps in the outline before you fill it in.

1. Click on the oval tool. Then, click on the middle option under the tool box. Draw ovals for the head, body and eyes.

2. Click on the brush and on a small brush style. Draw ears and a nose. Add pupils in the eyes. Draw the rest of the body.

3. Click on the eraser tool. Rub out any extra lines. Click on the paint can and click on a colour. Click on the drawing to fill it in.

To draw this comic strip, first draw some frames and then use the tips above to draw the mouse in different positions.

Draw and colour the cheese and the backgrounds last.

# Making a copy

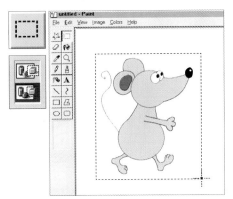

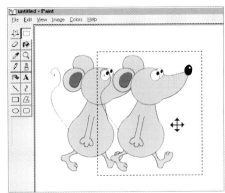

1. Click on the select tool. Click on the bottom option under the tool box. Pressing the left mouse button, drag a box around the drawing.

2. Position your pointer in the box and, holding the CTRL key down on your keyboard, drag the box. It will make a copy. Click outside the box.

3. You can drag the copy into another frame in your strip, and then change it. Use the eraser, brush and paint can tools to alter the picture.

# Turning heads

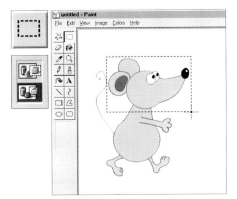

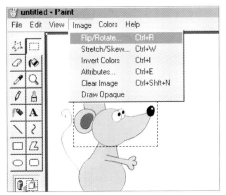

1. Click on the select tool. Click on the bottom option under the tool box. Pressing the left mouse button, drag a box around the mouse's head.

2. Click on *Image* at the top of the window. A list will appear. Click on *Flip/Rotate*. A box will appear. Click in the dot by *Flip horizontal*, and then click on *OK*.

3. The mouse's head will flip over. Pressing the left mouse button down, drag the head so it fits onto the body. Click outside the box to fix it in place.

Find out how to add a speech bubble on page 55.
Add the bubble before you colour the background.

★

# Drawing from life

To get cartoon ideas for how people stand, how they act or look in certain situations, it is a good idea to keep a little sketchbook with you. Make quick drawings of people around you at bus stops, in shopping centres, in parks or playgrounds.

Try to draw quick cartoons of the way people run.

Don't worry about drawing very accurately, sometimes a rough sketch can show more character.

Do scribbly drawings of the things people do while waiting for a bus.

If you are drawing someone close up, make sure you ask their permission first.

People standing at a bus stop can look bored, cold, relaxed or tense.

# Pulling faces

Many cartoonists keep a mirror by their drawing board. If they want to draw a cartoon of someone showing a particular emotion, and need to see what it would look like, they pull a face showing that emotion in the mirror. If you have a camera, you can also take pictures of friends pulling exaggerated faces to use as reference.

Take an online tutorial in how to draw expressions in a 'Manga' style (Japanese comic book style). Or, learn about caricatures and take a tutorial to draw some. For quick links to these Web sites, go to www.usborne-quicklinks.com

When someone is surprised, their eyebrows go up and their mouth opens wide.

When someone is grimacing, one eye shuts and their mouth slants to one side.

When someone is gleeful, their eyebrows go up and their mouth makes an open curve.

When someone is feeling thoughtful, they might look up and to one side.

When someone is shouting, their mouth opens very wide.

If someone feels suspicious, one eyebrow goes up and the other goes down.

# Gallery

Over the next four pages you can see a gallery of
cartoons, which were drawn or painted using
techniques and materials described in this book.
Look through the gallery for new ideas. You can
turn back to the pages mentioned to read more
about certain techniques.

Cartoon sausage dogs can be made
extra long, like this one. (See pages
16-17 for more dog characters.)

This giraffe was
drawn using
permanent pen
and watercolour
(see page 22).

The balloons were
painted on damp paper
letting the colours blur
together (see page 22).

These people were drawn using ideas
from pages 8-11. They were outlined
in permanent pen and painted
using watercolours (see
pages 22-23).

Take online cartooning lessons, including how to draw in a Japanese 'Manga' style, and look at famous cartoons. For links to these Web sites, go to **www.usborne-quicklinks.com**

The motion lines on these monkeys show that they are swinging (see page 36).

These people all have different-shaped faces (see pages 8-9). The scene was coloured using an effect similar to those described on page 26.

This boy was drawn in 'Manga' style. Manga is a Japanese comic book style.

This spider was painted using watercolours (see page 22).

Lines have been added here to show the impact of the girl kicking the ball (see pages 36-39).

This character looks a bit squashed because he's fallen over (see pages 38-39).

These shadows were created using shadow and colour effects like those on pages 21 and 26.

These hares were drawn on computer, using a program called Microsoft® Paint (see pages 52-57).

This speeding car has motion lines and puffs of smoke to show how fast it is going. You can see how to do these techniques on pages 36-37.

These faces were drawn showing different expressions (see page 6 and page 59).

This was drawn using pen and then painted using watercolours (see page 22).

A fairground can make an exciting setting for a comic strip. This wall was drawn showing perspective (see page 42-43).

This monster was drawn as an oval shape with arms and legs. It was painted with watercolours, using light and dark shades for the fur.

☞ Play cartoon games online. Draw cartoons using a simple online palette. Explore a cartoon world, or get some ideas for drawing cartoon backgrounds. For links to these Web sites, go to **www.usborne-quicklinks.com**

The clothes this man is wearing show that he is a cowboy (see page 12).

This cat was drawn using a similar technique to the animal characters on pages 16-17.

A castle is a good setting for a spooky cartoon. This scene uses colour effects to make it look spookier (see page 26).

These men all have the same body shape (see page 10-11), but their clothes make them look like different people.

This girl was drawn over and over in different positions to show her movements. This technique can be used in a comic, or in animation (see pages 50-51).

# Index

## Acknowledgements

Every effort has been made to trace the copyright holders of the material in this book. If any rights have been omitted, the publishers offer their sincere apologies and will rectify this in any subsequent editions following notification. The publishers are grateful to the following organizations and individuals for their contributions and permission to reproduce material:

Page 4 Bash Street Kids Summer Special 2002 ©D.C. Thomson & Co., Ltd; Dangermouse ©FremantleMedia Enterprises Ltd
Page 5 PEANUTS ©2001 United Features Syndicate, Inc; Mickey Mouse ©Disney
Page 10 Asterix and Obelix ©2002 LES EDITIONS ALBERT RENE/GOSCINNY–UDERZO; child (photograph) ©Digital Vision
Page 12 Desperate Dan ©D.C. Thomson & Co.,Ltd
Page 16 Count Duckula ©FremantleMedia Enterprises Ltd
Page 20 GARFIELD ©2000 Paws, Inc.
Page 30 Donald Duck ©Disney
Page 32 PEANUTS ©2001 United Features Syndicate, Inc.
Page 50 Popeye and Olive Oyl. Reprinted by special permission of King

Features Syndicate
Screen shots on pages 52-57 used with permission from Microsoft Corporation. Microsoft®, Microsoft® Windows® 95 and Microsoft® Paint are either registered Trade Marks or Trade Marks of Microsoft Corporation in the US and other countries. Quicktime is a Trade Mark of Apple Computer, Inc. Shockwave and Flash™ are Trade Marks of Macromedia, Inc, registered in the US and other countries. RealPlayer® is a Trade Mark of RealNetworks.

Series Editor: Fiona Watt
Art Director: Mary Cartwright
Picture researcher: Alice Pearcey
Thanks to Ben Denne for pulling faces and Brian Voakes for taking photos.

First published in 2002 by Usborne Publishing Ltd, 83-85 Saffron Hill, London EC1N 8RT, England. www.usborne.com

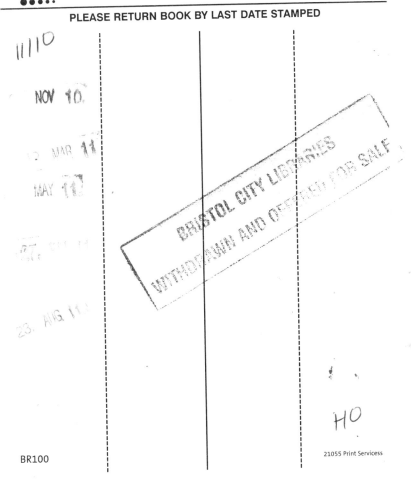